Lion Dreaming

Lion Dreaming

POEMS

Layered with old scars
The ghost of my missing hand
Reaches for a pen

Robert E. Rhodes

iUniverse, Inc.
New York Lincoln Shanghai

Lion Dreaming
POEMS

iUniverse books may be ordered through booksellers or by contacting:

iUniverse
2021 Pine Lake Road, Suite 100
Lincoln, NE 68512
www.iuniverse.com
1-800-Authors (1-800-288-4677)

ISBN: 978-0-595-47636-7 (pbk)
ISBN: 978-0-595-91900-0 (ebk)

Printed in the United States of America

This one is for Mimi and Karin and Julia and Laura and Aaron and Kim, sometimes in my poetry, always in my heart.

Contents

LION DREAMING

I am a lion dreaming
At home among elephants

I raise my massive head
In full grasp of the plain

Blood dries on my muzzle
From the fresh kill before me

When I open my jaws to roar
More blood drips from my rough, red tongue

My comely lioness arrives
To feed on parts I leave for her

I give her golden rump a swat
Which she's permitted to ignore

Nothing moves before I look
Without permission of my eyes

Not wind to blow, nor bird to fly
Not river to run, nor sun to shine

I wake up from lion dreaming
Caged by time in an old man's mind.

WEATHER REPORT

This morning in mist and rain
The muddy ship that is our home
Tosses on a piñon sea
Weeping windows blur our view
What look like dark approaching waves
Made ominous by moving clouds
Are foothills to a mountain range
Wind that kept us from our sleep
No longer bothers to disturb
Poorly fabricated dreams
Work their way through all we see
The sun itself does not intrude
That yesterday was in command
No more now than shadowed light
Against a sea of angry clouds
Arise my love and help me watch
Weathers contending to occur
Mountains that we trust to be
Flatly refuse to reappear
This morning in mist and rain
The muddy ship that is our home
Tosses on a piñon sea.

BEAUCATCHER

Before I knew of calendars
Beaucatcher Mountain was the way
I kept the time of year
I watched how the sun
Moved north along its ridge
Time to put my shoes away
And run barefoot over summer
Free as I would ever be
To taste of immortality.

SPRING MUSIC

Waking slowly from your sleep
You escape a troubled dream
Is it wind you hear blowing
Or is it music being played
Something that keeps repeating
Over and over low and clear
Demanding your attention
It's a dove you hear calling
Come to tell you spring is here.

SARABAND FOR BERGMAN

On Sundays Bergman went to church
And listened to his father preach
His father's God a God of hurt
And pain the swiftest way to teach

From his father Bergman learned
All the things that are not true
Trading on these memories
He pictured all he shouldn't do

Sleeping in the beds of others
He became both man and wife
Testing against the pain of love
Endless magnitudes of strife

Bergman dreamed when he was young
Of being bad before he died
And by the time he was old
Nothing bad was left untried.

MORNING COMES TO PORVENIR

Up among the tallest pines
Breezes make their morning way
A kind of music where they go
And gentle scenting of the air
First light catches in their limbs
Wind begins acceleration
On the peak the sun grows bright
Young trees closer to the ground
Chitchat as scrub oak will do
An early morning audience
True groundlings at play
Now the largest of the pines
Shake out their fullest limbs
Back and forth in winds they wave
Birds lift off to spread the news
Morning has come to Porvenir!
Blest be all who shelter here

OUR OLD KENTUCKY HOME

Someone burned down the boarding house
Long after Tom and the ladies left
Was it a lady with a match
Come to set some crime aright
Did someone wake her from her sleep
A boy with keys to all the rooms
Who felt compelled to be a man
And forced the lady to comply
She who had been forced before
Back at home behind the barn
Who rose at dawn to slip away
Called by Tom rhapsodically
A woman from the hot rich South
Who lost her mind at eighty-five
Came back and burned the damn place down!

MEMORIES OF GRAD SCHOOL

Her gloved hand rested
On the large thigh of Henry James
Who seemingly did not notice
Or if he did he never mentioned it
With all his many opportunities
What a sensibility
Wasted on a fictive world
We need waste no words
For James did not
On she who dared to test
Waters of a sea so vast
Where all our ancient wrecks
Lie barnacled with grief.

TRAVEL PLANS

I'd like to go to Provincetown
And see the place where Kunitz lives
If indeed he's still alive
Maybe buy a little house
In walking distance of the sea
I'm tired of being where I am
And even more of being who
My wife I know will go with me
She likes to go where things are quaint
Those places summer people go
Where they can walk and watch the birds
Kunitz they say is sometimes seen
Sitting looking out to sea
I think I'll go to Provincetown
Would you like to go with me?

AN ODE FOR THE COLLATERAL DEAD

Those who cry for victory
Every time the flag is raised
Should know by now how similar
Are tyrannies of appetite

These few hours liberty
Taken from the battlefield
Between years of constant war
Are all we'll ever know of peace

Any act can lead to war
Flags go up and so we fight
Anarchy should be declared
Our natural condition.

WHERE LOVE HAPPENS

Go to where love happens
At the vortex of desire
Go to where we gather close
As limb is folded over limb
Go to that place where love is joy
Until the day we realize
Love happens best in memory
The very love that taught us how
Yet no amount of having loved
Readies us for loss of love
Can you feel the tightness start
Care to share a broken heart?

ONCE I WELCOMED HOW A LEAF

Once I welcomed how a leaf
Looked to me at summer's end
Set free by an autumn breeze
Seeming to dance on broken wing
But I grow harder now to please
Less willing to find delight
When wind takes on its edge of cold
Forcing leaves in multitudes
Madly to disfigure air.

MY MISTRESS BEING OLD

My mistress being old
Wants to marry me
I that she so scorned
While with open arms
She welcomed all the rest
I who stood and waited
For an occasional kiss
Now have the old prize
The chalice but no wine
A piece to gather dust
And tell of old lovers
My faithful wait finished
I will wed her soon
And take a cosy cottage
Filled with loving care
Then when she is most content
I will reveal to her
My new and younger mistress
Who has some honey left
For an old bee like me
Oh then we will see
How my late mistress
Now my wife can herself endure
Endlessly lonely evenings
Spent waiting for one
To condescend to come.

TURTLEDOVE

Welcome back my turtledove
I hear such sorrow in your song
Is this so sad a place for you
The cage you left is ready still
Those sweet seeds you like to eat
Are waiting in your plastic cup
Sadly your friend's no longer here
I found his scattered feathers
Where the black cat likes to hide
You should know by now my dove
How cruel a place the world can be
Not safe at all for birds to fly
There I've bolted up your cage
I'll try to find another friend
To share in your captivity
I've spread fresh papers carefully
So you can comment on the news.

LETTING LOVE BE

Speak to her or let her be
Practiced words you've said before
That no one sane can quite believe
The very things she wants to hear
Ready when she turns her face
Looking straight into your soul
For something more than simple lies
Kiss her now or let her be
Touching is the door to love
And should she close her eyes at this
Reaching out for more of you
Little doubt the time has come
To chance the limits of desire
Love her now or let her be.

CUES FOR THE MARRIAGE SERVICE

Cue the people still arriving
To take their places in the church
Let the ceremony start
Lovers must be sanctified
Repeating all the holy vows
Cue the parents to their places
Bridegroom facing down the aisle
No chance of saying no
Cue the music to begin
Bride to start her stately march
Holding to her father's arm
Mother may softly cry
Cue Hymen, god of marriage,
To begin his exhortation:
"Swear this day to keep all vows
Instructing you in matrimony
As far as doing what with whom
Or be belled, booked and candled
Out the door and straight to hell!"
Cue the church bells now to loudly ring
Set lovers free for dallying.

ROETHKE MAKES A CALL

"A bathtub is no place to die"
Roethke telephoning Kunitz said
"The water is not adequate
To cover up my weighty self
Death requires a certain grace
Time's critical but so is place"
But Kunitz would not play the game
"I've been down those stairs myself
Father, they say, drank acid neat
But I prefer to wait my turn
I love flowers too much for that"
So Roethke chose a swimming pool
Reciting an unfinished poem
Drowning himself in imagery
Kunitz in his garden sat alone.

OVERTIME

We spend our lives in overtime
Never allowed to leave our seats
Never permitted to know the game

No quarters and no innings
Nor any points for practicing
Nets forbidden to be used

Though we're granted overtime
Sad to say we'll never win
Even should the game begin.

BORN EACH TIME WE WAKE

We are born each time we wake
One by one our loves depart
Stepping back into the grave
And we are left again alive

History happens while we sleep
But not as we remember it
The smallest piece of memory
Serves to mark a dream's return

Every time we close our eyes
We stand ready to arrive
Bag and baggage there we are
Back at some starting place

History happens while we sleep
We are born each time we wake
Every time we close our eyes
We step back into a grave.

DOG PARK

In the vast landfill of my mind
Fifty acres of buried trash
Under a covering of years
Where I go to walk the dog
Each morning closer to my last
I like to walk out here alone
But one old guy has made it first
His three dogs running back and forth
Forcing me from my favored path
To walk among iconic trash
Outliving bones of dinosaurs
But my dog straining at his leash
Is not impressed with cleverness
Or notices when I almost fall
All he can think about is dogs
He pulls me back along the ridge
To where it's said the Japanese
Once were kept in a prison camp
The bones of a few still buried here
Marked by a scattered pile of rocks.

EARLY MATTERS OF BELIEF

Part of me wanted to believe
When the announcer was saying
That at the very moment creatures
Were crawling out of weird machines
Killing everyone they came across
Stopping only to drink their blood
Caught up in the slaughtering
I could not tear myself away
And still today that part of me
Watches people being killed
By creatures sent to do them harm
Climbing out of strange machines
Destroying people I don't know
Reminding me why I first learned
The real joy of pretended fear
And feel it happening again.

I KNEW A LADY

I knew a very fat lady
Who had for loving one old cat
And when the poor cat died of cream
She dreamed it back and fed the dream
And when the fat old lady died
The dream cat sat and cried and cried.

REFLECTIONS OF AN OLD GOURMAND

I have never eaten of the crab
Nor tasted lobster thermidor
But I have eaten of the pig
And many times of the cow
But mostly of the fowl I've fed
So by digestive logic
A lot of me is piggish
A larger quantity is bull and most of me is fowl
But thank the good Transformer
I have never eaten of the crab.

CREATURES GIVEN UP TO LIGHT

We walked until the shadows
Seemed darker than the trees
Our arms like branches grew
Dampness hung upon our words

We had become the very thing
We thought to leave behind
In darkness darker than the night
Rooted down and reaching out

We are such things as earth creates
When earth itself is turned about
Pointed out beyond the stars
Creatures given up to light.

MOVING OUT

"I will not cut your bloody grass"
I whispered to the rising sun
Piling the children in the car
Racing out from behind the house
Catching the sagging clothesline
On the makeshift luggage rack
Feeling the snap that set us free
"What about your books," my wife shouted
"We have no room for books," I said
"What are we doing?" the oldest asked
"Moving out, my dear, moving out."

TROUBLE AT THE SUPERSTORE

I saw this happen on TV
Maybe you saw it too
About this soldier back from war
Working at a Superstore
Greeting people at the door
Putting stickers on Carry-ins
Sent home by his manager
For disarming a ten-year-old
Who brought in a plastic grenade
Because he said it didn't work
The soldier came back after lunch
Ready to go out on patrol
With a pistol in his hand
Searching people at the door
For anything that might blow up
The manager calls 911
Who sends a SWAT team to the store
Fully equipped to handle
Any person with a gun
The kid who collects shopping carts
Thinking the store under attack
Runs to Guns and Ammunition
To get bullets for the soldier's gun
A clerk brings a camera
And starts to video the scene
The manager is on the phone
Saying "There are no hostages
Customers are free to leave."
"The hell they are," the soldier says
Firing his pistol into the air

An old man collapses on the floor
"Medic!" the spacey soldier shouts
Thinking there's a soldier down
"I told my wife this Superstore
Would cause trouble in the town."
"Put the gun down, you stupid fool!"
Yells a big guy in charge of Meats
"Sarge! Is that you?" the soldier says
"Stand down before someone gets hurt!"
"There was a kid with a grenade.
He wanted his money back."
"Send him over to Returns.
Hope he brought in his receipt."
The soldier puts away his gun
The old man rises from the floor
The SWAT team has coffee and pie
Compliments of the Manager
Who quietly fires the soldier
Saying he's unfit to Greet
Wearing his country's uniform
In a Wal-Mart Superstore.

BUYING THE WIND

I am allowed to buy the wind
To use exactly as I please
Today I chose to write a poem
Can you feel the breezes blow
A little south but mostly east
My words are pointing straight at you
Can you feel the turning wheel
The energy begin to flow
I have no further need for coal
Nor pumping of an Arab oil
No my friend I buy the wind
All the power words require.

A SINGLE ROSE

I found the rose I gave to you
Lying where you let it fall
Recalling what you said to me
"However lovely one rose may be
A single rose is no bouquet"
While I pretended to agree
This is what I should have said
"The smallest joy that life provides
Should not be wasted in regret
The single rose is still a gift
And is in fact a small bouquet
A token of love's flowering"
But all of this was left unsaid
When you so lightly said to me
"However lovely a rose may be
A single rose is no bouquet."

CELEBRATING DIFFERENCE

Arbus the photographer
Who celebrates differences
Came to check on Eddie Carmel
To see if he would qualify

See him in his living room
Looming over his parents
A figure in a fairy tale
Who's been told he's grown too big

His mother looking up at him
Trying to believe it's possible
Father in his best black suit
Wishing he were someplace else

Diane Arbus checks the light
"Would you mind looking down at them?
Hold your cane off to the side.
One more now and then we are done."

You must have seen the picture
Eddie Carmel standing there
A very different kind of child
Not one we want to celebrate.

LA SALLE STREET STATION

The apple I saw
In the Automatic Chilled Fruit Machine
Of the La Salle Street Station
Was not the apple I got
From the Automatic Chilled Fruit Machine.

APPEARING TO SLEEP

The girl only appears to sleep
We know she is pretending
She's lying on her mother's couch
Arranged in a suggestive pose
Wearing what looks like a gown
Pulled down low to show her chest
She knows she is being watched
By her mother who is a pro
At lying there upon the couch
And the man who takes her picture
Who is inspired by little girls
They have been an hour at it
It is a question of the light
The mother says it's best to wait
The photographer doesn't mind
The girl is growing sleepy now
And forgets she must pretend
The sun grows brighter on the couch
As if to bless her innocence
Mother shakes the girl awake
Who once more appears to sleep
I saw this picture in a book
With this critical instruction
All art requires that we pretend
Watching makes our seeing real.

DUET WITH A PARROT

In the morning when I walk
I pass a parrot in his cage
A prettier bird I've never seen
He thinks me in a nearby tree
Back and forth we pass our notes
In the jungle we are born to
Silencing the other birds
Who will not risk our airy ire
He speaks of monkeys making noise
I say coyotes make that sound
Some days our whistling turns strange
We grow confused on which is who
He's the man who's walking by
I'm the parrot in the cage.

FROST AT RIPTON

Sitting there alone he writes
Hair tangled in the morning light
Waiting for a place to start
He is fixed in time and place
What he sees is what he feels
And what he feels is what he writes
Now he's moving to the task
Left hand striking up the beat
Right hand putting words into play
Line by line he scores the poem
Constructing as he wants it heard
Hair tangled in morning light
Sitting there alone he writes.

SOCIOLOGY OF SPRING

How cautiously this new spring comes
So little novelty of form
When just a twist of social thumbs
Could press it out into a norm

The fact that man has learned the grace
Of trusting spring to come at all
Displays within a springless race
A tolerance of nature's gall

As though to prove that spring is right
The same trees blunder into bloom
And flowers working day and night
Disrupt in rows a random room

The social arts thus trust to spring
The ways of making greenness rhyme
And learn the confidence a thing
Repays when left to sun and time.

THE SMILE OF ARTAUD

Madmen when they die
Sometimes seem to smile
As if in dying
Madness goes along
The smile of Artaud
Is a face in point
Said to be playing
Marat at the time
His death mask was cast
What a fixed revenge
Captured in that smile.

WINTER READING

Wearing transparent panties
And very tight boxer shorts
Members of the Nearly Naked
Society of Poets
Meet between the bronze lions
Of the public library
Where in summer tourists come
But alas it's winter now
Wind is blowing off the lake
Not a time for naked truth
Or poets huddled in a heap
Taking turns at speaking out
Pigeons watch from where they perch
Maintaining their innocence
But no human stops to hear
Sixteen naked poets read
Nor share their disfigurement.

SOLITUDES OF COLD

It seemed so simple to the eye
One lake with assorted ducks
Mountains white against the sky
In all that solitude of cold

Trees gone bare to blackest bark
Blending with the lake's dark shadows
One man walking all alone
In that stark solitude of gold

These few elements of life
Things that stand and walk and fly
Form a new complexity
Fixed in solitudes of cold.

CAREFUL LADIES WHAT YOU SAY

Careful ladies what you say
And whom you choose to say it to
Your lament may turn to gossip
Which repetition treats as true
That reaches those receptive ears
Of friends who meet to twist your words
Adding any necessary spice
Before they make of it a meal
Which they can serve up as their own
From recipes that you've provided
Then in weekly magazines
You find photos of your friends
Who've made a book of your mistakes
A movie due out in the spring
Garnished with their photographs
And no mention of you at all.

AWAKE TO WORLDS UNFOLDING

Awake to worlds unfolding
To sidewalks wet with morning rain
To just how thin a puddle is
When freckled out to dry.

Awake to how your fingers curl
Around the heavy hang of books,
The running jump before the bell
When every moment is your own.

Awake between the plodding lines
To see the way ideas grow;
Awake to worlds unfolding
Between the new syllables of time.

LINCOLN IN A LETTER TELLS

Lincoln in a letter tells
Why killing in war is no crime
War, he said, leads to confusion
Making thinking difficult
Which leads in turn to deception
And the necessity to kill
Or be oneself the one to die
Thus war's an act of self-defense
Dealt out in retaliation
Always on a battlefield
Where killings are deemed natural
That otherwise we call a crime.

ONE EVENING BACK IN THE STATES

One evening back in the states
I wondered why I ever left
I counted up my worries
Of things that happen anyway
Then subtracted my own neglects
Habits we make our lives from
And knew that I had come back too soon
All the reasons I had left
All the things I'd left undone
Nothing in me had changed at all
And even if I left again
I couldn't stay away for long
I counted up my worries
Of things that happen anyway
Subtracted my own neglects
Habits we make our lives from
One evening back in the states
Another evening in the states.

NOT ON MY BIRTHDAY!

Once in a neighbor's barn
The woman who was my mother
Took a switch to me.
Caught playing with other children
Whose parents she despised
She pulled me into the barn;
"You know I told you," she yelled
"Never to play with them again!"
Striking my naked legs
With every syllable
Forcing me to dance barefooted
Among piles of fresh manure.
"Please, Mama, please," I begged
"Not on my birthday!"
Years later she told the story
Repeating "Not on my birthday!"
And always getting a laugh.

MR EAVES

Mr. Eaves who practiced English
In the quiet of his room
Made an art of imitation

Many times I've passed his doorway
And heard him speaking out a line
Reciting to a record

Over and over heard him say
In an accent not his own
Gielgud perhaps or Burton

Heard him practicing alone
English as it should be spoken
In a deep and proper tone.

WHAT I WAS TOLD

I was told that God would listen
When I said my nightly prayers
But it wasn't God who listened
It was my aunts outside my door
Amazed what children would believe

I was told I had a father
A man that I had never seen
I asked God for my father's name
Something I had asked of Him before
But again He did not answer

I was told I had a mother
Who came to see me now and then
With a man who waited for her
Outside in a truck and trailer
Blowing his horn to call her out

"God," I asked, "Who is that driver?"
Causing my aunts to loudly laugh
"Could it be my father out there
Demanding that his son appear?"
God, if He knew, did not answer.

THIS WILL MAKE YOUR MOTHER ANGRY, JOHN

This will make your mother angry, John
No matter that you waited fifty years
To risk her unforgiving stare
Drinking somewhere by yourself
Just when things were going well
One drink too many as she told you
And there you are in Humpty Dumpty land
Trying for a graceful dive
Kicking out and falling free
Much too late for supper, John
Forever late for supper, John.

DANCING WITH THE DEVIL

In the cabin in the woods
See the doctor's daughter light
Seven candles in the darkness
For the seven kneeling farm girls
Come to learn the devil's dance
See her turning down the cross
Taking up the devil's pin
Waving it in candle smoke
She forms a black cat sleeping
"Sisters, sisters, raise your hands up
Say the devil comes to take me
Make me now his secret lover"
Farm girls say the wicked words
Doctor's daughter wakes the cat
And swings it by its long black tail
Until it spits into the darkness
She pokes its belly with her needle
Making it howl a hellish music
That all the farm girls dance to
One by one the devil takes them

Curing each one of any goodness
As they circle in their dancing
To the fury of the music
Doctor's Daughter begins to chant
"There are babies crying to be made
In the image of the devil
Say it now! Say his name!
You're the dancer! He's the dance!"
Farm girls give themselves to darkness
And to the joys of wickedness
Dancing wildly with the devil.

WALKING THE DOG

I have seen in the eyes of my love
Strange men walking little dogs
Fancy men in coats and ties
Swinging fancy walking sticks
Then I realize it's only me
Reflected there in her eyes
Swinging a fancy walking stick
Wearing a fancy coat and tie
Walking my dog in her eyes
The deep dark eyes of my love.

PICKING DAISIES

A crippled boy picks
Daisies from a pile of trash
Sunday's altarpiece:
"He loves me; He loves me not"
God must love you little child
Don't the daisies tell you so?

LIVING IN THE NOW

When lies are all we ever hear
Who's to say they are not so
Fear is what we have to share
When bravery becomes a crime

We can't discuss where we have been
And there's no chance of moving on
Denying what the future holds
There's only lots and lots of now

If yesterdays cannot be used
To teach us how mistakes are made
Our lives are free of consequence
Spent always in the present tense.

PAPA'S LUCK

No one ever mentioned luck
But in every house there hung
A picture of Jesus looking kind
And a dog howling at the moon
The dead all went to glory
The only luck they ever knew
And when the saints were marching by
We knew each one by name
Each one allowed a favored song
"He came to the garden alone
The dew was still on the roses"
Is something I remember
It was cold when Papa died
All the graves were humped with snow
His song does not come to me
But his pale face stays in my mind
And the slow, slow way he went
I fogged the window with my breath
Wrote the day of his dying down
And may have said a childish prayer;
The sickness that lifted Papa up
Freeing him from all his pain
May have been the only luck
Our poor Papa ever had.

DOING THE CROSSWORD

Over ocean routes the water nymphs
Transvaal the golden regions
Where Lear's three daughters rest.

"So be it!" cries Cyrus the Great
Named Bird by Gilbert and Sullivan
Small mocking unspiritual bird
Crossing crumb rivers to England.

Sailboating conjointly from this
Country of the northern river
As some shining kind of dancer
Ranging over the Wyoming crescent
Holding Hawaiian tubers like
A great lower limbed roofpart
Twisting the neck of a biblical king
Whose slangless nickname masticates
Now concluded divisions of pain.

FRETFUL HANDS

And then when dark is final
The hands refuse to stop
The thumbs begin to twiddle
Knuckles are made to pop

That's when worms come
Fingers come waving them in
Pointing out the tender places
With imitated gluttony

The nails start tracing out a map
Of the soul's supposed geography
Saving always to the last
The silent, disbelieving heart.

DAY OF THE DEAD

Men are digging a fountain
In the cemetery wall
Bone is striking against bone
Open a grave and set them free
This is their day to celebrate
Lay them out in proper order
Hang them upright in a cart
Roll them all around the town
Call the priest to come and bless them
Then put them back where they belong
In the cemetery wall.

RUTA IN SANTA FE

He stands on the edge of a field
Looking across into the trees
His canvas tied down with a rope
His easel anchored in the ground
He traces with an empty brush
A scene done many times before
Today he works against the wind
Siding as always with the trees
Back in his New York studio
A plane smashes old work apart
Burning the pieces he has done
All framed and ready for a show
While Ruta safe in Santa Fe
Lays out his palate for the day.

PAPA'S MIRACLE

As a child I learned to pray
Kneeling nightly by Papa's bed
Praying his sores would go away

Believing as a child believes
God would hear me as I prayed
And grant Papa his miracle

The night he died he said to me
"Do not pray to make me well
Death may be my miracle."

HOW THE LOTTERY BEGAN

He reached into his watch pocket
And handed me a dime
"Please, Mr. Rockefeller,
I'd rather have your house"
And that, my children
Is how the lottery began.

NORTH TO BOSTON

Running north to Boston
Made small by the night
Never so much alone
With only the sea for company
And the light of a distant star
Trying to outrun the storm
Sending waves up through the deck
Burying our running lights
In the spread of colored foam
Trailing out into a wake
The moon saw fit to light

Morning and the storm was worse
"Take her down," the Captain said
"Give the cooks a chance to serve"
The sea below is more than still
The storm raging right above
"Take her up," the Captain said
And back we went into the storm
"Set your engines all ahead"
Up and down we rode the waves
Submerging now and then to eat

If you must go north to Boston
Never go by submarine!

ROADSIDE ATTRACTIONS

It was silent when I stopped
Somewhere on a mountain road
Then listening I heard the birds
Insects in a swarm flew by
A beetle landed on my hood
Moving his legs like jointed oars
He crossed a waxy pond
Barely able to advance
In suddenness a blackbird came
Landing where the beetle moved
Snapping him up in her beak
Tiny legs still visible
Two gulps and it was gone
The bird looked to see
What objection I might have
And seeing none was itself
Swallowed up into the air.

LION OF LUZERN

On broken swords and bloody shields
Clearly marked with God's own sign
Lion rests his massive frame
Called upon to represent
Seven hundred fighting Swiss
The elite Praetorian Guard
Killed protecting a Christian king
Who, in fact, had run away
Lion seems somewhat ashamed
Caught defending God and France.

THINGS WE DO WHEN WE'RE ALONE

Things we do when we're alone
At moments when it matters least
Have little need for imagery
Or shifting ambiguity
That make a kind of may be so
For all the things that never were
Times like these require few words
Irony has let us down
Satire has a bitter smell
Discourse is at best a ruse
Pundits practice on TV
Whimsy does not stop the pain
Very few believe in God
Those who do refuse to share
Life itself's an iffy state
Thus we come to poetry
Things we do when we're alone
At moments when it matters least.

NIGHT CALLS

One night about two o'clock
My cell phone rang beside my bed
And I fumbled for it in the dark
Thinking it was my daughter
Who got me the cell phone
To find me when I am lost
Which happened in an airport once
But it was not she calling me
It was someone in Chicago
Looking for her daughter
Out too late it seemed
And who was very upset
That I answered my phone
"Is Clarisa with you?"
She demanded of me
"Who the hell are you," I said
"You sound like a white man!"
The woman said suspiciously
"And you sound black to me."
I replied in my southern drawl
"Put Clarisa on NOW!" she yelled
In a tone I do not condone
On my cellular telephone
Which I now used to turn her off
The next day I called my daughter
To tell her about my night call
She said I should complain
To the place she got the phone

So that is what I did
And they said it wasn't their fault
The number of my phone
Had been recycled
Part of a Chicago family plan
The next night the woman called
Looking for Clarisa again
I told her I was in Santa Fe
Had never met her daughter
And she better not call again
But she didn't believe me
And neither did my wife.

MAPPING THE PAST

Having touched the points in order
On the chart that lies unfolded
Between the days when payment falls
We drag out our memories
To make lament acceptable
Amazed to have survived at all
Endless acts of innocence
New islands of remembrance
Matter up from ocean floors
Starting at the peak we climb
Down as far as light will hold
Risking no sleep between the tides
For fear the moon will shake us free
To drift forever deep in stars.

SCHILLER'S SONG OF JOY

Slowly now the dying stops
A thing the dead will understand
Schiller are you watching now
Can you see their lovely souls?

Go among the enlisted men
Who died in sullen anger
In other seasons of despair
By now they all should know your song

Low voices are whispering "Hush!"
Bombs are falling somewhere near
We hear them as a muffled roar
Songs the dead have heard before

Slowly now the flags come down
Dead souls are free to start to sing
Schiller are you listening
Is that your song of joy we hear?

AUDEN

Here's old Auden in New York
Seen among the falling snow
As just another immigrant
Resolute of intellect
Bundled in his overcoat
On his way to buy the Times
Slowing up to strike a pose
Practicing his next routine
A Chaplin who forgot his hat.

THE CONVERSION OF GEORGE

It's said that Billy Graham
Brought George W to the Lord
Up at Kennebunkport, Maine
He taught George the words to say
Taught him how to kneel and pray
Gain forgiveness for his sins
And the Lord was pleased with George
And Billy told him he was saved
If he promised to be good
To go forth and sin no more
Thus salvation came to George
And he was filled with godliness
Given faith that he was right
To go among his fellow men
Spreading his new conviction
And God became his father
Saying, "Go out, George, and sin no more!"
Thus it came time to pass
George became a Governor
Then, by God, our President!
Since the day that he was saved
George it's said has never sinned
Living in a state of grace
He's never made one mistake
And always, always tells the truth
Just as Billy taught him to.

AVOIDING THE SAD THINGS

My mother writes that Uncle Ed
Has had a second heart attack
I mustn't mention sad things
Because they make him start to cry

She tells me that Aunt Hazel
Has bought my dying uncle
A 73 Chevy convertible
Although he cannot leave the Home

When last I saw Aunt Hazel
We talked about a chicken
She kept alive for fifteen years
Showing me the empty cage

"Eddie's doing better now
Since I put him in the Home"
Hazel said, drinking from a jar
Nodding where Ed used to sit

"Dear Uncle Ed," I write to him
"I hear you have a Chevy now"
And I don't mention the chicken
Or the empty cage on the porch.

ANOTHER WAL-MART WAR

"It's like fighting a war in Wal-Mart"
I hear this soldier say
Just then a kid with a bomb
Comes running down Aisle Two
Pushing people to the right and left
Shouting, "No God But Allah!"
Our sarge shouts back, "Bush!"
And we shoot twenty people
Just to bring the little prick down
Things happen very fast
When Wal-Mart has a war
He falls and the bomb explodes
Spreading freedom everywhere
We walk out without a scratch
At least that's what we tell the press
"Wal-Mart clean up on Aisle Two!"
I hear a soldier say.

THE ONLY CHILD

"The only child is a lonely child"
My Granny used to say
Who had six of her own
If you count the one who died
Me she called her only child
"You've got a lot of room," she said
"To do the things you have to do
There's no one to hold you back
You're free to be yourself"
Papa worked somewhere at night
I slept with Granny in her bed
Her back to me was always warm
"Don't forget to say your prayers
An only child must pray to God
Jesus was His only child"
Granny never said these things
But I did sleep with her at night
Her flannel gown my place to pray
Never lonely in her care.

.

A FLY AT THE WINDOW

A fly at the window
Makes motions on the glass
He eyes a grain of sugar
Resting near my coffee cup
Or is it that he watches me
Resenting my audacity
Making light of what I write
As something foreign to his taste.

NIGHT THOUGHTS

I do not mention God by name
Nor criticize his management
But still I wonder in the night
What the hell is going on
There's hungry children everywhere
And no one bothering to care
There's strange diseases of the blood
With cures most people can't afford
Poverty comes in black and white
Ashes of the dead come in gray
If heaven is so wonderful
Why does no one want to die
I do not mention God by name
Nor do I wish him to know mine
Yet I want something I can blame
For all these thoughts I have at night
These sad, sad thoughts I have at night.

AFTERLIFE

When your last breath has left you
That's the time decay begins
News is spread from cell to cell
Ruptured enzymes are set free
To eat away surrounding flesh
Bacteria races through the veins
To the lungs and to the heart
Then on out through arteries
To organs not yet consumed
The little left of what you were
If kept dry can be folded up
To fit into the drawer of time
And if lucky you may last
Longer than a thousand years
Dusted off and polished up
A grinning arrangement of bone.

978-0-595-47636-7
0-595-47636-8